Forecasting Disasters

BLIZZARDS

Trudy Becker

Copyright © 2026 by Apex Editions, Mendota Heights, MN 55120. All rights reserved. No part of this book may be reproduced or utilized in any form or by any means without written permission from the publisher.

Apex is distributed by North Star Editions:
sales@northstareditions.com | 888-417-0195

Produced for Apex by Red Line Editorial.

Photographs ©: Shutterstock Images, cover, 1, 4–5, 6–7, 8–9, 10–11, 12–13, 14–15, 16–17, 18–19, 30–31, 34–35, 44–45, 48–49, 58; Abe Fox/AP Images, 20–21; AR/AP Images, 22–23; AP Images, 24–25, 26–27; Wayne Bell/Star Tribune/Getty Images, 29; iStockphoto, 32–33, 52–53, 56–57; NASA, 36–37, 42–43, 50–51; Ron Frehm/AP Images, 38–39; Dave Chidley/The Canadian Press/AP Images, 41; Craig Ruttle/AP Images, 46–47; Andreas Arnold/picture-alliance/dpa/AP Images, 54–55

Library of Congress Control Number: 2025930289

ISBN
979-8-89250-659-5 (hardcover)
979-8-89250-694-6 (ebook pdf)
979-8-89250-677-9 (hosted ebook)

Printed in the United States of America
Mankato, MN
082025

NOTE TO PARENTS AND EDUCATORS

Apex books are designed to build literacy skills in striving readers. Exciting, high-interest content attracts and holds readers' attention. The text is carefully leveled to allow students to achieve success quickly.

TABLE OF CONTENTS

Chapter 1
WHITE SKY 4

Chapter 2
WHAT ARE BLIZZARDS? 10

Chapter 3
EARLY BLIZZARD FORECASTS 20

That's Wild!
HUNTING DISASTER 28

Chapter 4
MODERN METHODS 30

That's Wild!
SNOWMAGEDDON BLIZZARD 40

Chapter 5
MODELING BLIZZARDS 42

Chapter 6
INTO THE FUTURE 50

TIMELINE • 59
COMPREHENSION QUESTIONS • 60
GLOSSARY • 62
TO LEARN MORE • 63
ABOUT THE AUTHOR • 63
INDEX • 64

Chapter 1
WHITE SKY

A small car rushes down the highway. Outside, cold wind whips through the air. The wind shakes the car. Inside, a family looks up at the white sky. They are heading home after a trip. The dad has been driving for hours. But home is still far away.

Blowing snow can make the road hard to see.

On some highways, signs warn drivers of winter storms.

Wind rocks the car again. Thick snow starts to fall. The family watches the snow accumulate on the road. Suddenly, a loud alarm rings out. The mom grabs her phone. An emergency alert pops up on the screen. It's from the National Weather Service. The message warns people to get inside. A blizzard is on the way.

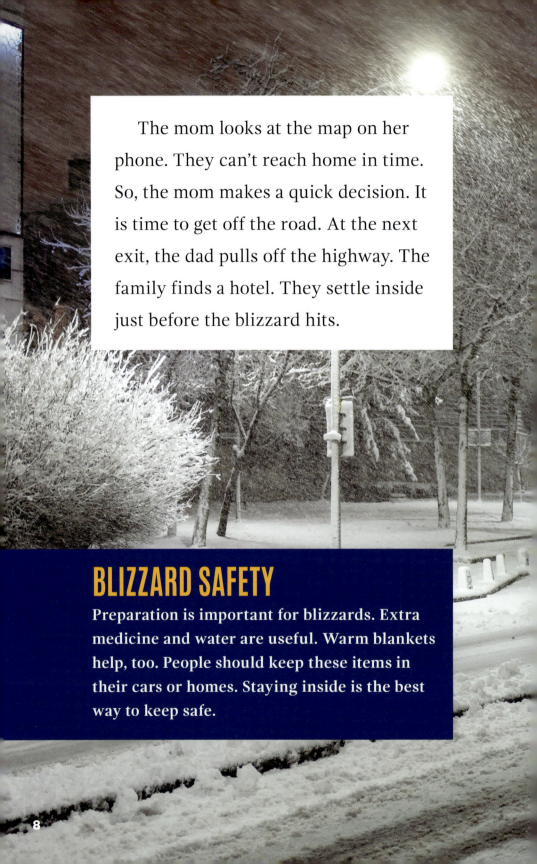

The mom looks at the map on her phone. They can't reach home in time. So, the mom makes a quick decision. It is time to get off the road. At the next exit, the dad pulls off the highway. The family finds a hotel. They settle inside just before the blizzard hits.

BLIZZARD SAFETY

Preparation is important for blizzards. Extra medicine and water are useful. Warm blankets help, too. People should keep these items in their cars or homes. Staying inside is the best way to keep safe.

Blizzards can make driving very dangerous.

Chapter 2
WHAT ARE BLIZZARDS?

A blizzard is a type of strong storm. It involves falling snow or snow that's already on the ground. To be a blizzard, a storm needs a few other features. The wind's speed must be above 35 miles per hour (56 km/h). Visibility must be less than 0.25 miles (0.4 km). And the storm must last more than three hours.

A whiteout happens when the sky and ground both look white, making it very hard to see.

During a blizzard, the temperature is usually below 10 degrees Fahrenheit (−12°C).

Blizzard conditions don't appear out of nowhere. Usually, blizzards happen if the temperature is already cold. Wind and humidity in the air are also needed. With those conditions in place, a blizzard may start to form. It may build up slowly over days.

NEW MEANING

The word *blizzard* wasn't always used for winter storms. In the past, *blizzard* meant a cannon shot. But in the 1870s, the word got a new meaning. A newspaper article called a storm a blizzard. The word became popular after that.

Blizzards can hit in many different places. But open, flat pieces of land in cold areas get the most blizzards. In the United States, the Midwest and Northeast often see blizzards. So do many parts of Canada. Some parts of Europe and Asia get blizzards, too.

AMERICAN BLIZZARDS

Blizzards are common in the United States. Since 2005, most states have seen at least one blizzard. Minnesota, North Dakota, and South Dakota get the most.

Blizzards are especially common in rural areas with few trees.

Heavy snow can cause the roofs of buildings to collapse.

Blizzards are powerful. Heavy snow can bring down power lines. Ice can freeze pipes. Strong winds tear pieces off buildings. If blizzards happen in the spring or fall, they can destroy crops. Also, snowdrifts block roads. People can't get to school or work. And businesses can't open. That means people lose money.

BLIZZARD TRAFFIC

In 2008, a series of ice storms hit China. The ice and blizzards arrived over a major holiday break. Millions of travelers were stranded. They were stuck on roads, in train stations, and at airports.

17

Blizzards can be dangerous. Slick roads and whiteouts lead to car crashes. And the cold itself is dangerous. People may get hypothermia or frostbite. The deadliest blizzard on record was in 1972. It happened in Iran. The blizzard killed 4,000 people.

Blizzards can cause drivers to spin off the road.

Chapter 3
EARLY BLIZZARD FORECASTS

In the past, blizzards were hard to predict. People didn't have enough technology to know when blizzards were coming. It was also harder to spread the word. People often had little warning. That problem happened in 1941 in Manitoba, Canada. A blizzard came so suddenly that people were still wearing spring clothes.

A blizzard in 1940 shut down the city of Boston, Massachusetts.

By the 1950s, scientist were using computers to predict the weather.

By the early 1900s, meteorologists were measuring many of the same things they do now. For example, they checked temperature and humidity. Then they spread that information. They sent telegrams. Or they put forecasts in newspapers. However, many measurements were taken just twice a day. And they were less accurate than they are now.

In the mid-1900s, it was hard for meteorologists to search through old information.

Early forecasters used past data, too. For example, if a storm arrived nearby, meteorologists checked records of similar storms. Those records helped them guess where the storm would go next. But forecasters often got it wrong.

EARLY TRACKING GROUPS

In 1849, the Smithsonian Institution started collecting weather data. It donated supplies for measuring. Volunteers across the country sent in their information. Later, the US government formed national weather organizations. The Signal Service was the first. It began tracking the weather in 1870. Eventually, the National Weather Service took over.

In 1888, a cold front came into the United States from Canada. Using past data, forecasters expected it to go out to sea. But instead, a huge blizzard hit New York City. People were unprepared. The city was buried in snow. Many telegraph lines went down. That made communication hard. But the mistake led to changes. City leaders decided to bury power lines. That helped people spread news during later blizzards.

BURIED CITY

The 1888 storm was intense. People tunneled through mountains of snow. They crossed the river on ice bridges. And they did everything possible to survive. Some New Yorkers burned tables for heat. Others caught and ate birds.

The 1888 blizzard in New York City caused damage to some buildings.

That's Wild!

HUNTING DISASTER

In 1940, a huge storm rushed into the Midwest. The arrival was quick. That led to a major problem. Weather services couldn't spread the word fast enough. Many duck hunters were out looking for birds. When the blizzard hit, it was too late for them to get inside. Temperatures dropped below freezing. More than 100 hunters died.

The disaster led to a key change in forecasting. Some weather offices extended their hours. They started staying open 24 hours a day.

People carry the body of a hunter who died in the 1940 blizzard.

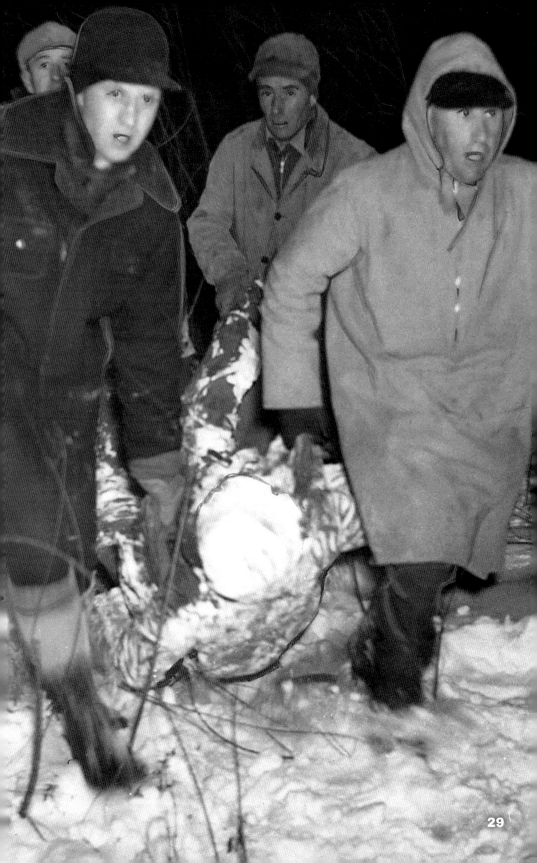

Chapter 4
MODERN METHODS

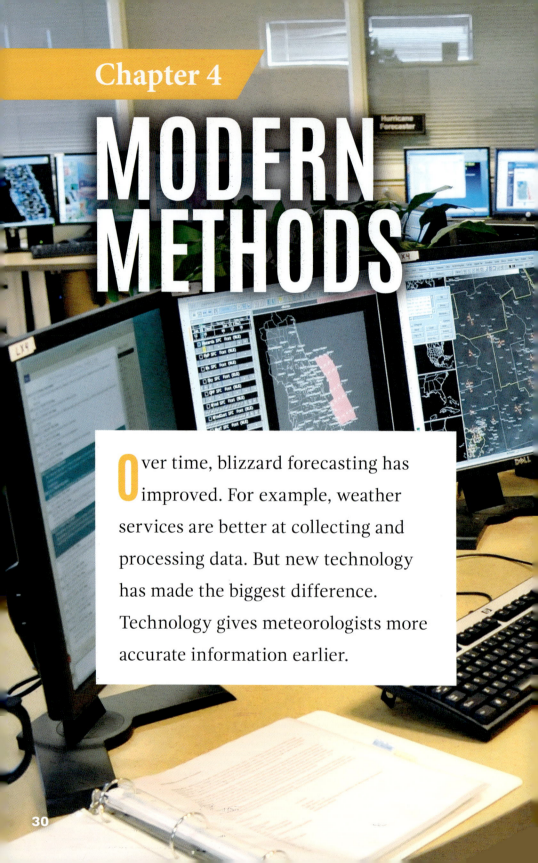

Over time, blizzard forecasting has improved. For example, weather services are better at collecting and processing data. But new technology has made the biggest difference. Technology gives meteorologists more accurate information earlier.

Modern computers make it easier for meteorologists to predict blizzards.

Radar is a key tool for blizzard forecasting. Radar works by sending out radio waves. The waves hit something. Then they bounce back. People can study the results and make predictions. The National Weather Service first used radar to watch the weather in 1942. The technology is useful for tracking precipitation.

TYPES OF RADAR

In 1992, people created a kind of radar called Doppler. Doppler helps show the direction the wind is moving. Later, dual polarization radar came. That radar identifies types of precipitation better.

A radar system is often covered by a dome, which protects the antenna from the weather.

People can stay safe by checking radar updates on their phones.

Precipitation and wind are key parts of blizzards. So, radar is useful to blizzard forecasters. Information from radar is also shown to the public. TV channels and websites display it. The radar shows changes by the hour. People can see when a blizzard will get stronger near them.

35

Satellites are another useful modern technology. Satellites are machines in space. They take images of Earth. Then the images are linked or looped together. That shows weather moving. For blizzards, satellites often help spot cloud patterns. The patterns can mean blizzards are coming.

A satellite image shows a huge winter storm.

TYPES OF WEATHER SATELLITES

There are two types of weather satellites. Polar satellites are one type. They show the full Earth twice a day. The other type is geostationary satellites. These satellites cover only half of Earth. But they provide images more often.

In 1993, the "Storm of the Century" arrived. The massive blizzard hit the eastern United States. Satellites tracked it in detail. Forecasters gave information five days ahead of time. That was a new record. The storm was terrible. More than 250 people died. But early warnings had saved many lives.

SPEEDY SPREAD

Forecasters need to share the information from radar and satellites. Over time, weather services tried different methods. They called news centers. They spread the word through radio and TV. Now, posting online is the fastest method.

The 1993 blizzard dropped heavy snow across much of the eastern United States.

That's Wild!

SNOWMAGEDDON BLIZZARD

In 2010, a storm hit Ontario, Canada. The storm lasted for 102 hours. Snow fell for 98 of those hours. The area got nearly 6 feet (2 m) of snow. That was a new record. The storm was known as "Snowmageddon."

But forecasters had warned about the blizzard. So, people had enough time to prepare. Public transportation shut down. The Canadian military came to help, too. Thanks to their preparation, Snowmageddon was just a big storm. It wasn't a human disaster.

School was canceled during the Snowmageddon blizzard.

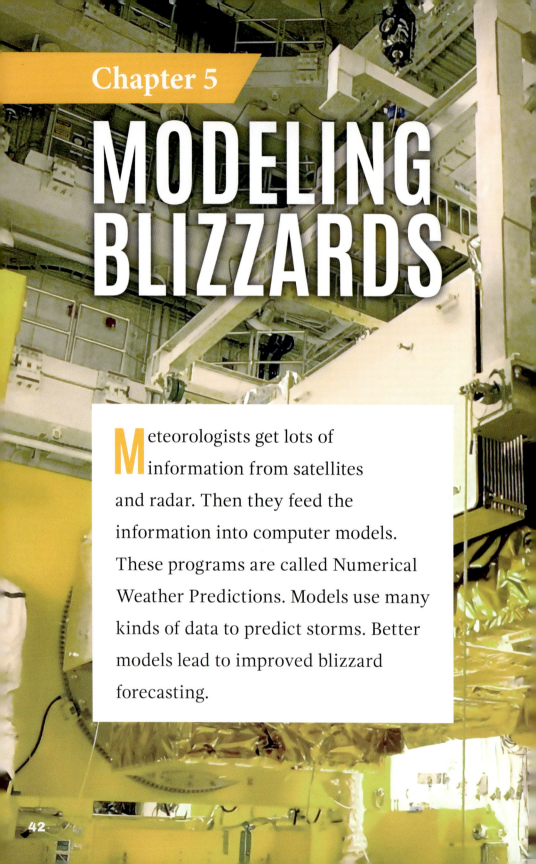

Chapter 5
MODELING BLIZZARDS

Meteorologists get lots of information from satellites and radar. Then they feed the information into computer models. These programs are called Numerical Weather Predictions. Models use many kinds of data to predict storms. Better models lead to improved blizzard forecasting.

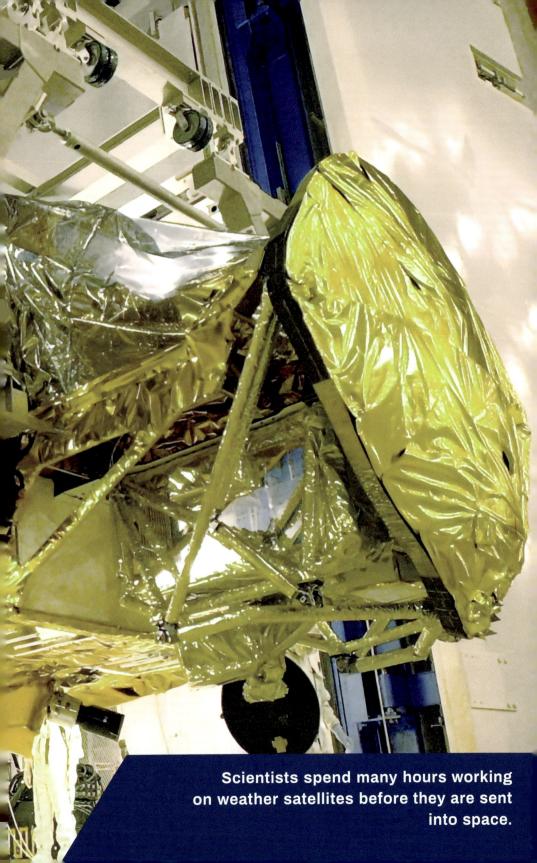

Scientists spend many hours working on weather satellites before they are sent into space.

Computer models run on code. Sometimes models show different weather results. Other times, many models predict the same thing. That happened in 2016. A blizzard hit the mid-Atlantic region of the United States. Results from several models agreed on its arrival time. People in the area got ready in time.

SUPERCOMPUTERS
Weather models need lots of energy to run. Scientists use some of the world's most powerful computers. The computers are fast. Some can do 100 trillion calculations per second.

Combining information helps make weather predictions more accurate.

45

Newer weather models make more specific predictions. For example, some examine smaller units of the atmosphere. That was useful for a 2022 blizzard in Buffalo, New York. The forecast helped people close businesses early. Many drivers got off the roads. Dozens of people died. But the forecast still saved lives.

WEATHER WORK

Governments run some weather services. Others are private businesses. AccuWeather is one example. In 2022, a blizzard hit the northeast United States. AccuWeather's predictions were very accurate. The service closely guessed the snow levels for several cities.

The city of Buffalo banned driving for several days during the 2022 storm.

To keep people safe, airlines often cancel flights during blizzards.

48

Models and other tools are useful. But a human touch is still important. In 2019, weather models said a blizzard was coming near Buffalo. They said it would hit south of the city. But meteorologists knew their models had been off in the past. So, they took the info and adjusted it. They correctly predicted the storm would hit the city straight on. The decision helped people prepare for the storm.

Chapter 6

INTO THE FUTURE

Blizzard forecasts have come a long way. But people are still trying to improve them. Mathematicians and scientists work on new technology. Computer scientists develop more code. And meteorologists find new ways to use all those tools.

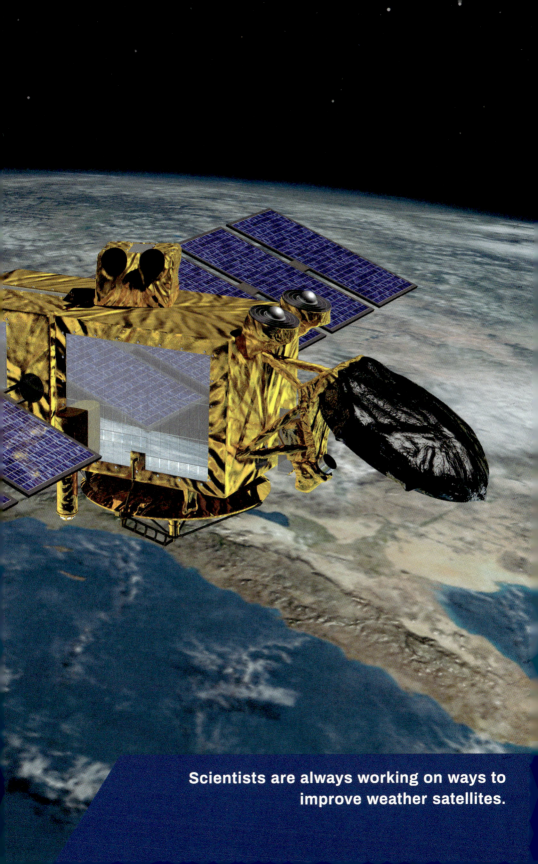

Scientists are always working on ways to improve weather satellites.

Some new technology improves forecast accuracy. For example, satellites have continued to advance. New satellite images show more detail. That is especially helpful when blizzards bring low visibility. Better radar is improving accuracy, too. New types give more detail about precipitation. Forecasters know what to expect during blizzards.

AHEAD OF TIME

It's usually easier to predict weather when a storm is close. But accurate forecast times are getting longer. In the 2020s, four-day forecasts were common. They were as accurate as one-day forecasts were in the 1990s.

As radar systems improve, scientists can predict storms more accurately.

Improved computer models help scientists make better forecasts.

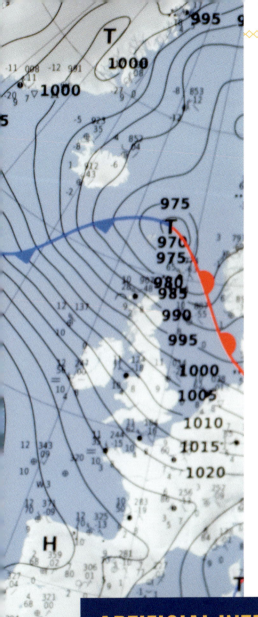

New technology also helps people make better forecasting decisions. For example, new computer models can do multiple forecasts for one storm. Experienced forecasters get more information from that. New scientific studies help, too. For example, some studies show how snow moves and melts. That helps forecasters read snowstorm radar.

ARTIFICIAL INTELLIGENCE

Artificial intelligence (AI) can also help forecasters. For example, GraphCast predicts weather up to 10 days ahead. Many scientists expect AI to become a bigger part of blizzard forecasting in the future.

Scientists and governments are improving communication, too. Stronger alert systems help. New systems involve technology that many people use. Alerts may reach all phones within a certain range. With fast alerts, new technology, and experienced meteorologists, more people can stay safe.

IPAWS

In 2011, the United States began a new alert system. It is called IPAWS. This system sends alerts at national, state, and local levels. The information comes to people's phones, radios, and TVs.

Alerts on phones can help people reach safety more quickly.

TIMELINE

1849 — The Smithsonian Institution starts collecting weather data.

1888 — A major blizzard hits New York City.

1940 — A huge blizzard rushes into the Midwest.

1941 — A blizzard arrives suddenly in Manitoba, Canada. People are still in spring clothes when it hits.

1972 — A deadly blizzard in Iran kills 4,000 people.

1993 — Satellites help people prepare for the "Storm of the Century."

2008 — Ice storms strand travelers in China.

2010 — A blizzard in Ontario, Canada, drops snow for 98 hours over a 102-hour period.

2011 — The IPAWS alert system begins.

2022 — Forecasters correctly predict a major blizzard in Buffalo, New York.

COMPREHENSION QUESTIONS

Write your answers on a separate piece of paper.

1. Write a few sentences describing the features of a blizzard.

2. What would you do if you knew a blizzard was coming? Why?

3. When did the deadliest blizzard in history happen?
    - A. 1941
    - B. 1972
    - C. 2010

4. Why might meteorologists make changes to the predictions of weather models?
    - A. Weather models are never correct.
    - B. Meteorologists have extra knowledge and experience.
    - C. Meteorologists don't know how to read the models.

5. What does **intense** mean in this book?

*The 1888 storm was **intense**. People tunneled through mountains of snow. They crossed the river on ice bridges.*

- A. harsh
- B. small
- C. easy

6. What does **extended** mean in this book?

*The disaster led to a key change in forecasting. Some weather offices **extended** their hours. They started staying open 24 hours a day.*

- A. eased
- B. shortened
- C. increased

Answer key on page 64.

GLOSSARY

accumulate
Slowly build up.

artificial intelligence
Computer systems that can learn and change without following new instructions.

atmosphere
The layers of air that surround Earth.

code
Instructions that tell a computer or device what to do.

data
Information collected to study or track something.

frostbite
Damage to skin or other body parts, caused by freezing.

humidity
The amount of moisture in the air.

hypothermia
When a person's body temperature drops dangerously low.

meteorologists
Scientists who study the weather.

precipitation
Water that falls to the ground as rain, sleet, hail, or snow.

visibility
How well and how far people can see.

TO LEARN MORE

BOOKS

Becker, Trudy. *Texas Ice Storms*. Apex Editions, 2024.

Dalgleish, Sharon. *Blizzards*. Apex Editions, 2023.

Taylor, Charlotte. *Blustery Blizzards*. Gareth Stevens, 2023.

ONLINE RESOURCES

Visit **www.apexeditions.com** to find links and resources related to this title.

ABOUT THE AUTHOR

Trudy Becker lives in Minneapolis, Minnesota. She likes books and exploring new places. She also loves snow.

INDEX

AccuWeather, 46
alert systems, 7, 56
artificial intelligence, 55

Buffalo, New York, 46, 49

Canada, 14, 20, 26, 40
China, 17
code, 44, 50
computer models, 42, 44, 46, 49, 55
crops, 17

Doppler, 32

frostbite, 18

GraphCast, 55

humidity, 13, 23
hypothermia, 18

IPAWS, 56

mathematicians, 50
meteorologists, 23, 25, 30, 49, 50, 56

National Weather Service, 7, 25, 32
New York City, 26
Numerical Weather Predictions, 42

phones, 7–8, 56

radar, 32, 35, 38, 42, 52, 55

satellites, 36–38, 42, 52
Signal Service, 25
Smithsonian Institution, 25
Snowmageddon, 40
Storm of the Century, 38

whiteouts, 18
wind, 4, 7, 10, 13, 17, 32, 35

ANSWER KEY:
1. Answers will vary; 2. Answers will vary; 3. B; 4. B; 5. A; 6. C